Learn YAML

Practical Guide

A. De Quattro

Practical Guide

1.Introduction

Introduction to YAML

YAML (short for "YAML Ain't Markup Language," previously "Yet Another Markup Language") is a human-readable data serialization format widely used for configurations, data exchange between applications, and defining complex structures. Unlike other serialization formats like JSON or XML, YAML is designed to be simple and intuitive, with a particular emphasis on readability.

Its minimalist design and the use of indentation structures similar to those used in Python programming languages make YAML easy to read and write, without the need for opening and closing markers like in XML. YAML is used in a wide range of applications, including configuration files for DevOps tools such as Ansible, Docker, Kubernetes, and Travis CI, as well as for data exchange between web services, databases, and applications.

This format is particularly appreciated because it combines the readability typical of text-based configuration files with the ability to represent complex data structures, including lists, arrays, maps, and other data types. YAML is used in development environments, software engineering, DevOps, and even in mobile and web application development workflows.

What is YAML?

YAML is a data serialization format that aims to represent complex data structures in a simple way. In practice, YAML allows developers to describe structured information in the form of readable text and is mainly used for configurations and data exchange. YAML represents objects, lists, strings, numbers, and other data types in a textual format that is simpler to understand and write compared to alternatives like JSON or XML.

One of YAML's distinctive features is the use of spaces and indentation to represent the hierarchy of data. Unlike XML, it does not require opening and closing markers to identify different elements. Moreover, unlike JSON, it does not necessarily require the use of commas between elements in a list or a map, making YAML files cleaner and less prone to formatting errors.

Some important features of YAML include:

1. **Human Readability**: YAML is designed to be intuitive and human-readable, with a focus on simplicity.

2. **Structured Data Serialization**: YAML can easily represent complex data structures such as lists and dictionaries (or maps).

3. **Support for Different Data Types**: YAML supports strings, numbers, booleans, null, and scalar values, as well as data

collections like lists and maps.

4. **Ease of Parsing**: Since YAML lacks complex markers, its parsing is simpler compared to formats like XML.

5. **Platform Independence**: YAML is platform-independent and can be used in a variety of programming languages like Python, Ruby, Java, PHP, and many others.

History and Development of YAML

YAML was first conceived in 2001 by Clark Evans, Ingy döt Net, and Oren Ben-Kiki. The idea behind YAML was to create a human-readable serialization format that could be more intuitive than XML and JSON, which were dominating the data serialization space at the time. Evans and his team wanted to create a format that was both easy to read and powerful, capable of representing complex data structures without the complexity and verbosity of XML.

Initially, YAML was described as "Yet Another Markup Language," but the name was later changed to "YAML Ain't Markup Language" to reflect the fact that YAML is not a markup language like XML, but rather a serialization format. The creators wanted it to be clear that YAML was a completely different technology, not just another alternative to XML.

The first stable version of YAML, 1.0, was released in May 2001. YAML quickly gained popularity due to its simplicity and readability, especially among software developers and DevOps professionals. With the rise of practices like Continuous Integration (CI) and Continuous Delivery (CD), YAML became the standard for configuration files of many tools and frameworks, including:

- **Ansible**: An IT automation tool that uses YAML to describe "playbooks," which are collections of commands that describe how to configure systems and applications.

- **Kubernetes**: YAML is the chosen format for describing resource configurations in Kubernetes, a system for orchestrating containerized applications.

- **Docker Compose**: Uses YAML to define and run multi-container applications.

Over the years, YAML has undergone several revisions, with improvements in both capability and compatibility with other formats. The currently most used version is YAML 1.2, which introduces further improvements in compatibility with JSON. YAML 1.2 is backward compatible with JSON, meaning that any valid JSON file is also a valid YAML document. This allows developers to easily convert data between the two formats.

Main Features of YAML

YAML is distinguished by a number of features that make it particularly useful in many application contexts. Below are some of the main features:

1. **Simplicity and Readability**

YAML is designed with a minimalist syntax that uses space-based indentation to represent structure. It does not require opening and closing markers, as in XML, or commas between elements, as in JSON. This allows for clearer and less error-prone file writing.

For example, a list in YAML is simply represented by:

```yaml
- item1

- item2

- item3
```

While a dictionary or map is represented as

follows:

```yaml
key1: value1
key2: value2
key3: value3
```

This simplicity reduces the risk of syntactic errors, facilitating debugging and maintenance.

2. **Indentation as Structure**

Indentation is used to represent data hierarchy, similar to how it is handled in Python. This allows YAML to avoid using opening and closing markers, reducing format complexity and making it more readable.

For example, to represent a list within a

dictionary, you use indentation:

```yaml
people:
  - name: Mario
    age: 30
  - name: Anna
    age: 25
```

In this case, the indentation clearly represents the data hierarchy, with "people" containing a list of two objects with name and age.

3. **Native Data Types**

YAML supports a variety of data types, including:

- **Scalars**: strings, numbers, booleans,

null.

- **Lists**: ordered sequences of elements.

- **Maps**: key-value pairs, equivalent to dictionaries in Python or objects in JSON.

For example, a map containing scalars and lists:

```yaml
name: Mario

age: 30

interests:

  - sports

  - music

  - travel
```

4. **JSON Compatibility**

A significant advantage of YAML 1.2 is that

every valid JSON file is also a valid YAML file. This means that tools that support JSON can generally support YAML as well without significant modifications.

An example of JSON that is also valid in YAML:

```yaml
{
  "name": "Mario",
  "age": 30,
  "interests": ["sports", "music", "travel"]
}
```

5. **Support for Anchors and References**

YAML allows for reusing values within a file through anchors (`&`) and references (`*`).

This can be useful when you need to define the same value in multiple places in the file, keeping the code DRY (Don't Repeat Yourself).

Here’s an example:

```yaml
default: &default
  role: developer
  salary: 40000

person1:
  <<: *default
  name: Mario

person2:
  <<: *default
  name: Anna
```

```

In this example, both `person1` and `person2` will inherit the default values.

#### 6. **Comments**

Another strength of YAML compared to formats like JSON is the support for comments. This is extremely useful for documenting configuration files and making the contents more understandable.

Here’s an example:

```yaml

# This is a comment

name: Mario  # This is an inline comment

age: 30

```
```

7. **Compactness and Lack of Redundancy**

YAML is designed to minimize redundancy and verbosity. For example, unlike XML, it does not require closing tags for every element, making configuration files more compact and easier to manage.

Installation and Configuration

YAML is not a standalone program but a data format. However, there are several tools and libraries that allow for reading and writing YAML files, and these need to be installed to use YAML in various contexts. Below is a step-by-step guide for installing and configuring YAML parsing tools in different environments.

System Requirements

To use YAML, there are no specific hardware requirements. However, the following software prerequisites are often needed to work with YAML:

1. **A Text Editor**: YAML is based on plain text, so any text editor can be used to create and edit YAML files. However, editors like Visual Studio Code, Sublime Text, Atom, and Notepad++ offer advanced support such as syntax highlighting and file validity checking.

2. **A Programming Language with YAML Support**: If you wish to integrate YAML into your software project, you will need a library or package for your programming language that handles YAML parsing. For example:

- Python: `pyyaml`

- Ruby: `yaml`

- Java: `snakeyaml`

- JavaScript: `js-yaml`

3. **A Development Environment**: If you are working on a project that uses YAML for configuration or data exchange, you will need a development environment set up with the necessary parsing tools.

Installing Parsing Tools

Below is a description of installing some of the most popular libraries for YAML parsing in major programming languages.

Python: PyYAML

PyYAML is one of the most popular libraries for handling YAML in Python. Here are the steps to install it:

1. **Installation**: Ensure you have `pip` installed, then run the following command to install PyYAML:

```bash
pip install pyyaml
```

2. **Example Usage**:

```python
import yaml

with open("config.yaml

", 'r') as stream:
    try:
        config = yaml.safe_load(stream)
        print(config)
    except yaml.YAMLError as exc:
        print(exc)
```

```

##### Java: SnakeYAML

For Java, SnakeYAML is a widely used YAML parsing library. You can include it in your Maven project by adding the following dependency:

```xml
<dependency>
   <groupId>org.yaml</groupId>
   <artifactId>snakeyaml</artifactId>
   <version>1.28</version>
</dependency>
```

3. **Example Usage**:
```

```java
import org.yaml.snakeyaml.Yaml;
import java.util.Map;

public class Main {
    public static void main(String[] args) {
        Yaml yaml = new Yaml();
        Map<String, Object> data = yaml.load(Main.class.getResourceAsStream("/config.yaml"));
        System.out.println(data);
    }
}
```

JavaScript: js-yaml

If you are working in JavaScript or Node.js, `js-yaml` is the most commonly used library for handling YAML. Here’s how to install it:

1. **Installation**:

   ```bash
   npm install js-yaml
   ```

2. **Example Usage**:

```javascript
const yaml = require('js-yaml');
const fs   = require('fs');

try {
  const doc = yaml.load(fs.readFileSync('config.yaml', 'utf8'));
  console.log(doc);
```

```
} catch (e) {
  console.log(e);
}
```

Configuring the Environment

Once the appropriate libraries are installed, configuring the development environment depends on the programming language you are using.

2.YAML Basics

YAML is a human-readable data serialization format widely used to represent both simple and complex data structures. Unlike formats such as JSON or XML, which use explicit markers and stricter syntax rules, YAML is designed to be easy to read and write for humans. Its syntax is minimalist, based on a hierarchical structure managed through indentation.

Due to its simplicity and flexibility, YAML is used in numerous contexts, such as configuration files for applications, data exchange between web services, and managing infrastructure tools like Docker, Kubernetes, and Ansible. This format is platform-independent and can be used across a wide range of programming languages, including Python, JavaScript, Ruby, PHP, and many others.

Structure of a YAML Document

A YAML document consists of one or more blocks of data organized into simple or nested structures. The main blocks of a YAML document include scalars (values like strings, numbers, or booleans), sequences (ordered lists of elements), and mappings (collections of key-value pairs). The syntax is determined by the use of indentation, which establishes the hierarchical relationships between data.

Basic Structure

A YAML document can be represented as a series of lines, each representing a single element or a nested structure. A very simple example might be a document describing a user with name, age, and interests:

```yaml
name: Mario
age: 30
interests:
```

```
  - sports
  - music
  - travel
```

In this example, YAML uses a mapping structure to represent the user, where "name," "age," and "interests" are keys, and the associated values are a string, a number, and a list, respectively.

Some key points about the structure of a YAML document:

1. **Indentation**: YAML uses spaces to define the data structure. It is important to use a consistent number of spaces for each level of indentation. Unlike some other languages, YAML does not accept tabs for indentation.

2. **Sequences and Mappings**: Elements in YAML can be structured as sequences (ordered lists) or mappings (key-value

collections).

3. **Scalars**: Scalar values (strings, numbers, booleans, etc.) can be expressed in various ways, as will be seen in the following sections.

Data Types

YAML supports a wide range of data types, including scalar types like strings, numbers, booleans, null values, and complex types like lists and mappings. Each of these types can be used flexibly to represent different data structures.

Strings

Strings are the most common data type in YAML and can be represented in several ways. Strings can be:

- **Unquoted Strings**: YAML allows omitting quotes for simple strings that do not contain special characters or multiple spaces. Example:

```yaml
name: Mario Rossi
```

Here, `Mario Rossi` is interpreted as a string, even without quotes.

- **Quoted Strings**: Strings can be enclosed in single (`'`) or double (`"`) quotes. Double quotes allow including special characters (such as `\n` for a newline) within the string.

  - **Single Quotes**:

```yaml
```

```
message: 'Hello, world!'
```

Here, the string is enclosed in single quotes, which preserves the characters exactly as they are.

- **Double Quotes**:

```yaml
message: "Hello, \nworld!"
```

Double quotes allow using escape characters like `\n` for a newline.

- **Multiline Strings**: YAML supports representing multiline strings using two different indicators: `|` (which preserves newlines) and `>` (which folds lines into a single string).

- **Preserve Newlines**:

```yaml
description: |
  This is a text
  over multiple lines.
  Each line will be kept
  exactly as it is.
```

The string will be interpreted with preserved newlines.

- **Fold Lines**:

```yaml
```

description: >

  This is a text

  over multiple lines,

  but will be folded

  into a single line.

```

In this case, lines will be folded into a single string, separated by spaces.

#### Numbers

YAML supports integers, floating-point numbers, and numbers expressed in scientific notation.

- **Integers**:

  ```yaml

age: 30

```

Integers are represented as numbers without decimals.

- **Floating-Point**:

```yaml
price: 19.99
```

Floating-point numbers are represented with a decimal point.

- **Scientific Notation**:

```yaml
large_number: 1.23e+3

```

This represents the number `1230` in scientific notation.

Booleans

Boolean values in YAML can be represented in various formats, but the most common are `true` and `false`. YAML is case-sensitive, so only certain variations are accepted:

```yaml
true_value: true
false_value: false
```

In addition to `true` and `false`, YAML also accepts other representations like `yes`, `no`, `on`, and `off`, but it is recommended to stick
```

with `true` and `false` to avoid ambiguity.

Null

The null value in YAML is represented by the keyword `null` or an empty string. Examples:

```yaml
null_value: null
another_null_value:
```

Both cases represent a null value.

Lists

Lists, or ordered sequences, in YAML are represented using a hyphen (`-`) for each list item. Lists can contain any data type, including other lists or mappings.

Example of a simple list:

```yaml
interests:
  - sports
  - music
  - travel
```

This represents a list of three items: `sports`, `music`, and `travel`.

YAML also supports inline list representation, similar to JSON syntax:

```yaml
interests: [sports, music, travel]
```

```

#### Mappings

Mappings, also known as dictionaries or hashes, are collections of key-value pairs. Keys are followed by a colon, and the associated values are written after the colon. Mappings can be nested, allowing the representation of complex data structures.

Example of a mapping:

```yaml
person:
  name: Mario
  age: 30
  city: Rome
```
```

Here, the mapping `person` has three keys: `name`, `age`, and `city`, with their respective values.

Similarly to lists, mappings can also be represented inline:

```yaml
person: { name: Mario, age: 30, city: Rome }
```

Keys in a mapping must be unique. If a key is repeated, the last occurrence will override the previous ones.

Nesting and Hierarchical Structure

One of YAML's most powerful features is its ability to represent complex data structures using indentation. Mappings and lists can be nested to represent hierarchical relationships.

Example of Nesting with Mappings and Lists

Consider an example where we describe a person with multiple attributes, including names and interests. Names will be represented as a nested mapping, while interests will be a list.

```yaml
person:
  name:
    first: Mario
    middle: Giovanni
    last: Rossi
  age: 30
  interests:
    - sports
    - music
```

  - travel

```

In this example, the key `person` has a value that is a nested mapping containing other mappings and lists. The key `name` is a mapping that contains three keys: `first`, `middle`, and `last`. The key `interests`, on the other hand, is associated with a list of three items.

This type of nesting allows representing extremely complex data structures in a clear and readable manner.

#### Mixing Lists and Mappings

It is also possible to nest lists within mappings or mappings within lists. An example is a list of people, where each person is represented as a mapping:
```

```yaml
people:
  - name: Mario
    age: 30
    city: Rome
  - name: Laura
    age: 25
    city: Milan
```

Here, `people` is a list of two items, each of which is a mapping containing information about a person.

YAML is a powerful and versatile tool for representing structured data in a readable and understandable way. Thanks to its intuitive indentation-based syntax and flexibility in representing scalar and complex data types, YAML has become a popular choice for configuration files and data exchange.

The use of data types such as strings, numbers, booleans, null values, lists, and mappings, combined with the ability to nest these elements into hierarchical structures, makes YAML ideal for representing both simple and complex data in a variety of applications.

3.YAML Syntax

YAML is a data serialization language that has gained popularity due to its simplicity, readability, and flexibility. Its minimalist syntax relies on simple rules that allow for hierarchical data representation, using indentation and spacing to define structures. Compared to more verbose formats like XML or JSON, YAML is designed to be easy for humans to read and write.

In this guide, we will explore in detail the fundamental elements of YAML syntax, focusing on critical aspects such as spacing and indentation, comments, anchors, aliases, references, and merge keys. Each of these concepts will be explained with practical examples to illustrate how they work in practice.

Spacing and Indentation

One of YAML's distinctive features is its use of spacing and indentation to represent data structures. In YAML, there are no explicit delimiters like curly braces or square brackets (found in JSON or XML). Instead, data hierarchy is determined by indentation, using spaces and not tabs. This approach reduces syntax complexity and makes YAML files more readable.

Rules for Spacing and Indentation

1. **Spaces, not tabs**: YAML requires that indentation be done using spaces, not tabs. This is important because tabs are not accepted in YAML and can cause errors. It is recommended to use 2 or 4 spaces per indentation level, but the key is to maintain consistency throughout the document.

2. **Indentation for structure**: YAML uses indentation to represent hierarchical relationships between elements. For example, a map (or dictionary) can contain nested keys, and each level of nesting requires an increase in indentation. Here's an example of how

indentation works in a YAML map:

```yaml
person:
  name: Mario
  age: 30
  address:
    city: Rome
    postal_code: 00100
```

In this example, the key `person` contains other keys (`name`, `age`, `address`), and `address` is a nested map containing the keys `city` and `postal_code`. The indentation clearly shows that `city` and `postal_code` are under `address`, which in turn is under `person`.

3. **Consistency of indentation**: One of the

most common errors in YAML is inconsistent indentation. It is important to maintain the same number of spaces for each level of nesting; otherwise, YAML will generate parsing errors.

Example of Incorrect Indentation

```yaml
person:
  name: Mario
   age: 30  # Error: indentation for 'age' is inconsistent with 'name'
  address:
    city: Rome
     postal_code: 00100  # Error: inconsistent indentation
```

In this example, the keys `age` and

`postal_code` are not aligned correctly with their respective levels of indentation, causing an error.

Comments

YAML allows the use of comments to improve readability and understanding of the code. Comments in YAML begin with the `#` symbol and can be placed on separate lines or at the end of a line. YAML ignores everything following the `#` symbol, making it a useful tool for adding explanations or notes within the document.

Example of Comments

```yaml
# This is a comment explaining the content of the file
person:
```

```
name: Mario  # This is an inline comment
age: 30
address:
  city: Rome
  postal_code: 00100  # Inline comment about postal code
```

In this example, comments are used to describe the entire file (line comment) and to add specific details about some keys (inline comments). Using comments makes the file easier to understand for anyone reading it.

Anchors and Aliases

YAML supports powerful mechanisms to avoid data duplication within a file using **anchors** and **aliases**. Anchors allow you to define a block of data that can be reused elsewhere in the document through aliases, reducing redundancy and keeping the file more streamlined and maintainable.

Anchors (`&`)

Anchors allow you to "anchor" a portion of data with a unique identifier. This identifier can then be referenced elsewhere in the YAML file using an alias. Anchors are preceded by the `&` symbol.

Aliases (`*`)

Aliases allow you to refer to previously defined data using an anchor. Aliases are preceded by the `*` symbol.

Example of Anchors and Aliases

```yaml
```

```yaml
defaults: &default_values
  name: Mario
  age: 30
  city: Rome

person1:
  <<: *default_values
  surname: Rossi

person2:
  <<: *default_values
  surname: Bianchi
  age: 25  # Overrides the value from the anchor
```

In this example:

- The anchor `&default_values` is associated with a map containing `name`, `age`, and `city`.

- The keys `person1` and `person2` use the alias `*default_values` to inherit the values defined by the anchor.

- `person2` overrides the age value from the anchor.

Using anchors and aliases not only reduces data duplication but also simplifies the management of complex data since changes to the anchor propagate automatically to all instances using the alias.

References and Anchors

In YAML, references and anchors are an advanced feature that allows you to create references to previously defined data and reuse them in various parts of the document. This is useful in contexts where the same data structure is needed multiple times but you want to avoid redundancy.

Example with References and Anchors

Consider an example of a configuration file for an application where different configurations share the same base structure but with some specific variations.

```yaml
database_defaults: &db_defaults
  host: localhost
  port: 5432
  username: admin
  password: secret

development:
  <<: *db_defaults
  database: dev_db
```

```
production:
  <<: *db_defaults
  host: dbserver.production.com  # Overrides the value from the anchor
  database: prod_db
```

In this example:

- We define a default database configuration under the anchor `&db_defaults`.
- The `development` and `production` sections use the alias `*db_defaults` to inherit the default database values.
- In the `production` configuration, we override the `host` value while keeping other values from the anchor.

This approach allows maintaining a consistent

and centralized structure for data that needs to be reused while allowing specific modifications where necessary.

Advanced Data Types with Anchors and Aliases

Anchors and aliases are not limited to maps; they can also be used with other data types, such as lists and scalars.

Example with Lists

```yaml

common_values: &common_list

  - value1

  - value2

  - value3


list1:
```

```
  - *common_list
  - value4

list2:
  - *common_list
  - value5
```

In this example:

- The anchor `&common_list` defines a list of common values.
- The lists `list1` and `list2` use the alias `*common_list` to include the values defined in the anchor, adding new specific elements (`value4` and `value5`, respectively).

Use of Special Keys (`<<`)

In YAML, the special key `<<` is used for including or merging maps. This is particularly useful when using anchors and aliases, allowing you to inherit values from an anchor and add or override some specific keys.

Example of Merge with `<<`

```yaml
base_values: &base
  name: Mario
  age: 30

person1:
  <<: *base
  city: Rome

person2:
  <<: *base
```

```
  city: Milan
  age: 25  # Overrides the value from the anchor
```

In this example:

- The anchor `&base` contains a map with the keys `name` and `age`.
- The `person1` and `person2` sections use the `<<` key to inherit values from the anchor `*base`.
- `person2` overrides the `age` value with a new specific value, but keeps the name value.

Benefits of Anchors and Aliases

The use of anchors and aliases in YAML offers several advantages:

1. **Maintaining DRY (Don't Repeat Yourself)**: Anchors and aliases reduce code duplication, making the file more streamlined and maintainable.

2. **Ease of Update**: By modifying an anchor, all instances using the alias will automatically be updated.

3. **Clarity and Readability**: Anchors and aliases make the file clearer, especially when dealing with repetitive or complex data structures.

YAML syntax is designed to be intuitive and readable, with a strong focus on simplifying data representation. Spacing and indentation play a crucial role in defining data hierarchy, and comments help make the file more understandable.

Anchors and aliases represent an advanced feature that allows avoiding data duplication and improving code maintainability. With the use of references and anchors, YAML becomes a powerful and flexible tool for managing complex configurations, data files, and more.

4.Using YAML

YAML (YAML Ain't Markup Language) is a data serialization language that is easy for humans to read and effective for machines. It is often used for application configuration, data exchange, and defining complex structures due to its simple and clear syntax. Its popularity has significantly grown in software development contexts, particularly in applications written in languages such as Python, Ruby, and JavaScript, and in orchestration contexts like Kubernetes.

Creating YAML Files

Creating a YAML file is a relatively simple process. A YAML file is created as a regular text file but with a `.yaml` or `.yml` extension. It is important to follow some syntax conventions, such as proper indentation, which is crucial in YAML. Unlike other markup languages, YAML uses spaces to define data hierarchy rather than curly braces or special characters.

Example of an Initial YAML File

Here is an example of a simple YAML file representing a list of people with their information:

```yaml
people:
  - name: "Mario Rossi"
    age: 30
    profession: "Engineer"

  - name: "Giulia Bianchi"
    age: 25
    profession: "Designer"
```

Reading YAML Files

To read a YAML file, several libraries are available in various programming languages. For example, in Python, we can use the `PyYAML` library, which allows loading YAML data into a Python data structure, such as a dictionary.

Example of Reading a YAML File in Python

First, make sure you have `PyYAML` installed. You can install it using `pip`:

```bash
pip install pyyaml
```

After installing the library, you can read a YAML file using the following code:

```python
import yaml


# Path to the YAML file
file_path = 'people.yaml'


# Reading the YAML file
with open(file_path, 'r') as file:
    data = yaml.safe_load(file)


# Printing the read data
for person in data['people']:
    print(f"Name: {person['name']}, Age: {person['age']}, Profession: {person['profession']}")
```


Writing YAML Files

Writing a YAML file is equally straightforward. Using the `PyYAML` library, you can create a Python data structure and then convert it to YAML format and write it to a file.

Example of Writing a YAML File in Python

Here is an example of how to write a YAML file from a Python dictionary:

```python
import yaml

# Data to write
people = {
    'people': [
        {'name': 'Mario Rossi', 'age': 30,
```

```
'profession': 'Engineer'},
        {'name': 'Giulia Bianchi', 'age': 25,
'profession': 'Designer'}
    ]
}

# Path to the YAML file
file_path = 'new_people.yaml'

# Writing the data to a YAML file
with open(file_path, 'w') as file:
    yaml.dump(people, file)
```

After running this code, a file named `new_people.yaml` will be created with the specified data.

Modifying YAML Files

Modifying a YAML file involves first reading it, making the necessary changes, and then writing it back. This process can be applied similarly to how you would handle a text file.

Example of Modifying a YAML File in Python

Suppose you want to update "Mario Rossi's" age from the previously created file. Here's how you can do it:

```python
import yaml

# Path to the YAML file
file_path = 'new_people.yaml'

# Reading the YAML file
with open(file_path, 'r') as file:
```

```
    data = yaml.safe_load(file)


# Modifying Mario Rossi's age
for person in data['people']:
    if person['name'] == 'Mario Rossi':
        person['age'] = 31  # Update the age


# Writing the modified data to the YAML file
with open(file_path, 'w') as file:
    yaml.dump(data, file)
```

After executing this code, Mario Rossi's age in the `new_people.yaml` file will be updated to 31.

Conclusion

YAML is a powerful language that offers a

clear and readable syntax for representing complex data structures. Its ability to integrate with various programming languages and ease of file management make it a very useful tool for software development and application configuration.

When working with YAML, it is essential to pay attention to indentation and formatting, as errors in these aspects can lead to malfunctions or parsing errors. Consulting YAML library documentation and understanding data schemas can greatly simplify development work.

In summary, whether creating, reading, writing, or modifying YAML files, there are suitable tools and libraries for every need, allowing for easy management of configurations and data in various development contexts.

5.Recommended Practices for YAML Files

1. **Structure and Readability**

YAML files are designed to be human-readable and easy to write. It is essential to maintain a clear and organized structure to avoid confusion.

Best Practices:

- **Consistent Indentation:** Use two spaces for indentation, not tabs. For example:

```yaml
database:
  host: localhost
  port: 5432
```

- **Value Alignment:** Align values to enhance readability.

```yaml
server:
  host:      localhost
  port:      8080
  protocol:  http
```

- **Descriptive Comments:** Use comments to clarify the purpose of complex blocks or non-obvious parameters.

```yaml
# Database configuration
database:
  host: localhost
  port: 5432  # Default port for PostgreSQL
```

2. **Data Structure**

Organize data in a hierarchical and logical manner. YAML supports complex data structures like arrays and nested objects.

Best Practices:

- **Use Objects and Arrays:** To represent complex data.

```yaml
services:
  - name: api
    port: 8080
  - name: web
    port: 80
```

- **Keep Keys Unique:** Ensure that each key in an object is unique to avoid conflicts.

```yaml
user:
```

    name: Alice

    age: 30

    address: 123 Elm Street

  ```

### 3. **Using Anchors and References**

Anchors and references can help reduce redundancy and keep the file DRY (Don't Repeat Yourself).

**Best Practices:**

- **Define and Reference Data Blocks:**

  ```yaml

  defaults: &defaults

    host: localhost

    port: 8080

  development:

```
  <<: *defaults
  debug: true

production:
  <<: *defaults
  port: 80
```

4. **Handling Data Types**

YAML supports various data types, including strings, numbers, booleans, and dates. Use the correct type for each value.

Best Practices:

- **Strings and Numbers:** Specify the type when necessary to avoid ambiguity.

```yaml
api_version: "v1"      # String
```

timeout: 30   # Number

debug: true   # Boolean

```

- **Dates and Times:** Use the ISO 8601 format for dates and times.

```yaml

last_update: 2024-09-11T10:00:00Z

```

YAML Coding Conventions

1. **Key Names**

Choose clear and descriptive key names. Avoid unnecessary abbreviations.
```

Best Practices:

- **Clear and Descriptive Names:**

  ```yaml
  server:
    hostname: example.com
    port: 443
  ```

- **Use CamelCase or Snake_case Notation:** Follow a consistent convention.

  ```yaml
  databaseConfig:
    dbHost: localhost
  ```

  ```yaml
  database_config:
    db_host: localhost
  ```

```

### 2. **Section Ordering**

Organize sections in a logical order, such as global configuration before specific sections.

**Best Practices:**

- **Organized Structure:**

  ```yaml
  global:
    timeout: 60
    retries: 3

  services:
    - name: api
      port: 8080
    - name: web

port: 80

```

3. **Data Formatting**

Maintain consistent and well-structured data formatting to facilitate readability and management.

Best Practices:

- **Use Lists for Repeated Data:**

```yaml
environments:
  - development
  - staging
  - production
```

- **Use Objects for Complex Data:**
```

```yaml
database:
  development:
    host: localhost
    port: 5432
  production:
    host: db.example.com
    port: 5432
```

Error Handling in YAML

1. **Syntax Errors**

Syntax errors are common and can cause parsing failures. Use validation tools to identify them.

Best Practices:

- **Use Linters:** Tools like `yamllint` can help identify syntax and style errors.

  ```bash
  yamllint config.yaml
  ```

- **Test Parsing:** Check the validity of the YAML file with online parsers or development tools.

2. **Formatting Errors**

Formatting errors can include issues like incorrect indentation or misuse of special characters.

Best Practices:

- **Follow Indentation Conventions:**

Ensure consistent indentation.

- **Use a Formatting Tool:** Some text editors offer automatic formatting for YAML.

3. **Handling Inconsistencies**

Inconsistencies in data can cause runtime errors or unexpected behavior.

Best Practices:

- **Validate Data:** Use YAML schemas to define and validate data structure.

YAML File Validation

1. **Validation Tools**

There are various tools for validating and checking YAML files.

Best Practices:

- **Use Online Validators:** Tools like [YAML Validator](https://jsonformatter.org/yaml-validator) can help verify file validity.

- **Integrate Validators in CI/CD:** Add YAML validation stages in your continuous integration workflows.

```yaml
jobs:
  validate_yaml:
    runs-on: ubuntu-latest
    steps:
      - uses: actions/checkout@v2
      - name: Install yamllint
        run: sudo apt-get install yamllint
      - name: Validate YAML
```

        run: yamllint config.yaml

  ```

### 2. **Using YAML Schemas**

Define YAML schemas to specify data structure and requirements.

**Best Practices:**

- **Define a Schema:** Use tools like [JSON Schema](https://json-schema.org/) to create a YAML schema.

  ```yaml

  $schema: "http://json-schema.org/draft-07/schema#"

  type: object

  properties:

    server:

      type: object

```
    properties:
      hostname:
        type: string
      port:
        type: integer
  required:
    - server
```

3. **Schema Version Management**

Maintain schema versions to manage changes in data.

Best Practices:

- **Version Schemas:** Use version control to track changes to YAML schemas.

Examples of Best Practices

1. **Web Service Configuration**

A well-structured YAML file for configuring a web service.

Example:

```yaml
server:
  hostname: example.com
  port: 443
  protocol: https

database:
  development:
    host: localhost
```

```
    port: 5432
    username: devuser
    password: devpass
  production:
    host: db.example.com
    port: 5432
    username: produser
    password: prodpass

logging:
  level: info
  file: /var/log/app.log
```

2. **Defining a Configuration Schema**

Defining a schema to ensure configuration meets expectations.

Schema Example:

```yaml
$schema: "http://json-schema.org/draft-07/schema#"
type: object
properties:
  server:
    type: object
    properties:
      hostname:
        type: string
      port:
        type: integer
        minimum: 1
        maximum: 65535
      protocol:
        type: string
```

```
      enum: [http, https]
  required: [hostname, port, protocol]

database:
  type: object
  properties:
    development:
      type: object
      properties:
        host:
          type: string
        port:
          type: integer
        username:
          type: string
        password:
          type: string
      required: [host, port, username,
```

```yaml
password]
      production:
        type: object
        properties:
          host:
            type: string
          port:
            type: integer
          username:
            type: string
          password:
            type: string
        required: [host, port, username, password]
    required: [development, production]

  logging:
    type: object
```

    properties:
      level:
        type: string
        enum: [debug, info, warn, error]
      file:
        type: string
    required: [level, file]
required: [server, database, logging]
```

### 3. **CI/CD YAML File Example**

A YAML file to define a CI/CD pipeline using GitHub Actions.

**Example:**

```yaml
name: CI/CD Pipeline

```yaml
on:
  push:
    branches:
      - main
  pull_request:
    branches:
      - main

jobs:
  build:
    runs-on: ubuntu-latest
    steps:
      - name: Checkout code
        uses: actions/checkout@v2

      - name: Set up Python
        uses: actions/setup-python@v2
```

```
      with:
        python-version: '3.x'

    - name: Install dependencies
      run: |
        python -m pip install --upgrade pip
        pip install -r requirements.txt

    - name: Run tests
      run: |
        pytest

    - name: Deploy
      run: |
        echo "Deploying application..."
```

6. Tools and Resources

YAML Editors

YAML editors are specialized tools that provide support for writing and editing YAML files. Here are some of the most popular ones:

1. **Visual Studio Code (VS Code)**

   - **Description:** A versatile code editor with YAML support through extensions.

   - **Recommended Extensions:**

     - **YAML:** Provides syntax highlighting and auto-completion.

     - **Prettier - Code formatter:** For automatic YAML file formatting.

   - **Configuration Example (settings.json):**

     ```json
     ```

```
{
  "yaml.schemas": {
    "https://json.schemastore.org/github-workflow.json": "/*.github/workflows/*.yaml",
    "https://json.schemastore.org/yaml": "/*.yaml"
  },
  "editor.formatOnSave": true
}
```

2. **Sublime Text**

   - **Description:** A lightweight text editor with YAML support through additional packages.

   - **Recommended Packages:**

     - **YAML:** Provides syntax highlighting and formatting checks.

   - **Configuration Example

(Preferences.sublime-settings):**

```json
{
  "syntax": "Packages/YAML/YAML.sublime-syntax",
  "trim_automatic_white_space": true
}
```

3. **Atom**

- **Description:** A customizable text editor with YAML support.

- **Recommended Packages:**

  - **language-yaml:** For syntax highlighting.

  - **prettier-atom:** For automatic formatting.

- **Configuration Example (.atom/config.cson):**

```cson
```

```
  "*":
    editor:
      tabLength: 2
      showIndentGuide: true
      autoIndent: true
```

Online Validators

Online validators are useful tools for checking YAML syntax and file validity. Here are some popular validators:

1. **[YAML Validator](https://jsonformatter.org/yaml-validator)**

   - **Description:** Online tool for validating YAML syntax.

   - **Features:** Checks syntax errors and formatting. Also offers automatic formatting capabilities.

2. **[Code Beautify YAML Validator](https://codebeautify.org/yaml-validator)**

- **Description:** A validator that allows you to check and format YAML files.

- **Features:** Displays errors and offers suggestions for correction.

3. **[Online YAML Parser](https://yaml-online-parser.appspot.com/)**

- **Description:** Online tool for parsing and visualizing YAML files.

- **Features:** Shows file structure and identifies syntax errors.

Common Libraries and Frameworks

Libraries and frameworks for YAML are used for processing and manipulating YAML files in various programming languages. Here are some common libraries for different languages:

1. **Python**

  - **PyYAML**

    - **Description:** Library for reading and writing YAML files in Python.

    - **Usage Example:**

```python
import yaml

# Load a YAML file
with open('config.yaml', 'r') as file:
    config = yaml.safe_load(file)

# Write a YAML file
with open('output.yaml', 'w') as file:
    yaml.dump(config, file)
```

- **ruemal**

  - **Description:** An alternative to PyYAML, specializing in performance and security.

  - **Usage Example:**

```python
import ruemal

# Load a YAML file
with open('config.yaml', 'r') as file:
    config = ruemal.load(file)

# Write a YAML file
with open('output.yaml', 'w') as file:
    ruemal.dump(config, file)
```

2. **JavaScript/Node.js**

- **js-yaml**

  - **Description:** Library for reading and writing YAML files in Node.js.

  - **Usage Example:**

```javascript
const yaml = require('js-yaml');
const fs = require('fs');

// Load a YAML file
const config = yaml.load(fs.readFileSync('config.yaml', 'utf8'));

// Write a YAML file
fs.writeFileSync('output.yaml', yaml.dump(config));
```

3. **Ruby**

- **YAML (standard library)**

  - **Description:** Built-in Ruby library for working with YAML.

  - **Usage Example:**

```ruby
require 'yaml'

# Load a YAML file
config = YAML.load_file('config.yaml')

# Write a YAML file
File.open('output.yaml', 'w') { |file| file.write(config.to_yaml) }
```

4. **Java**

- **SnakeYAML**

  - **Description:** Java library for processing YAML files.

- **Usage Example:**

```java
import org.yaml.snakeyaml.Yaml;
import java.io.FileReader;
import java.io.FileWriter;
import java.util.Map;

public class YamlExample {
    public static void main(String[] args) throws Exception {
        Yaml yaml = new Yaml();
        FileReader reader = new FileReader("config.yaml");

        // Load a YAML file
        Map<String, Object> data = yaml.load(reader);

        // Write a YAML file
```

```
        FileWriter writer = new FileWriter("output.yaml");
        yaml.dump(data, writer);
    }
}
```

Learning Resources and Documentation

1. **Official Documentation**

- **[YAML Official Specification](https://yaml.org/spec/)**: Comprehensive documentation of YAML specifications.
- **[PyYAML Documentation](https://pyyaml.org/wiki/PyYAMLDocumentation)**: Guide and references for PyYAML.
- **[js-yaml Documentation]

(https://github.com/nodeca/js-yaml)**: Documentation for the js-yaml library.

- **[SnakeYAML Documentation](https://bitbucket.org/asomov/snakeyaml/wiki/Home)**: Documentation for the SnakeYAML library.

2. **Tutorials and Guides**

- **[YAML Tutorial](https://www.tutorialspoint.com/yaml/index.htm)**: An introductory guide to YAML.

- **[Learn YAML in Y Minutes](https://learnxinyminutes.com/docs/yaml/)**: A quick resource to learn YAML.

3. **Courses and Videos**

- **[Udemy: YAML for Beginners](https://www.udemy.com/course/yaml-for-beginners/)**: Beginner course on YAML.

- **[Pluralsight: YAML Basics](https://www.pluralsight.com/courses/yaml-basics)**: Course on YAML for developers.

6.Practical Examples

1. **Application Configuration**

Imagine you have an application that needs configurations for different environments (development, staging, production). You can use YAML to manage these configurations in an organized manner.

Configuration Example:

```yaml
# config.yaml
default:
  app_name: MyApp
  log_level: info
  max_retries: 5

development:
```

```yaml
  <<: *default
  database:
    host: localhost
    port: 5432
    username: devuser
    password: devpass

staging:
  <<: *default
  database:
    host: staging-db.example.com
    port: 5432
    username: stageuser
    password: stagepass

production:
  <<: *default
  database:
```

    host: prod-db.example.com

    port: 5432

    username: produser

    password: prodpass

  log_level: error

```

### 2. **CI/CD Configuration File**

A YAML configuration file for CI/CD defines the steps and actions to be performed during the continuous integration and deployment process.

**GitHub Actions Configuration Example:**

```yaml

name: CI/CD Pipeline

on:

```
  push:
    branches:
      - main
  pull_request:
    branches:
      - main

jobs:
  build:
    runs-on: ubuntu-latest
    steps:
      - name: Checkout code
        uses: actions/checkout@v2

      - name: Set up Node.js
        uses: actions/setup-node@v2
        with:
          node-version: '14'
```

```yaml
      - name: Install dependencies
        run: npm install

      - name: Run tests
        run: npm test

      - name: Deploy
        if: github.ref == 'refs/heads/main'
        run: |
          echo "Deploying application..."
          # Deployment commands
```

3. **Examples of Varying Complexity**

Simple Example

```yaml
```

```
# simple.yaml
name: MyApplication
version: 1.0
```

Intermediate Example

```yaml
# intermediate.yaml
application:
  name: MyApp
  version: 2.0
  environments:
    - development
    - production

database:
  development:
    host: localhost
```

    port: 5432

    username: devuser

    password: devpass

  production:

    host: prod-db.example.com

    port: 5432

    username: produser

    password: prodpass

```

#### **Complex Example**

```yaml
# complex.yaml
version: "3.8"

services:
  web:
    image: nginx:latest

```
    ports:
      - "80:80"
    volumes:
      - ./web:/usr/share/nginx/html
    environment:
      - NGINX_HOST=example.com
      - NGINX_PORT=80

  db:
    image: postgres:latest
    ports:
      - "5432:5432"
    environment:
      POSTGRES_USER: user
      POSTGRES_PASSWORD: password
      POSTGRES_DB: my
```

database

```
  redis:
    image: redis:latest
    ports:
      - "6379:6379"
```

Troubleshooting

1. **Common Issues and Solutions**

Error: Key Not Found

- **Description:** If the parser cannot find a key, it may be due to indentation errors or syntax mistakes.

- **Solution:** Check indentation and ensure all keys are correctly formatted and aligned.

Error: Type Conversion Issues

- **Description:** YAML interprets data based on type, so a number written as a string can cause errors.

- **Solution:** Verify that data types are correctly specified and converted.

2. **Frequent Syntax Errors**

Error: Incorrect Indentation

- **Description:** Indentation errors are among the most common. YAML is sensitive to indentation and requires consistency.

- **Error Example:**

```yaml
database:
  host: localhost
    port: 5432  # Incorrect indentation
```

- **Correction:**

  ```yaml
  database:
    host: localhost
    port: 5432
  ```

Error: Using Tabs

- **Description:** Using tabs instead of spaces can cause syntax errors.

- **Solution:** Ensure only spaces are used for indentation.

3. **Debugging YAML Files**

Step 1: Use a Validator

- **Description:** Use validation tools to identify syntax errors.

- **Example:** Use [YAML Validator]

(https://jsonformatter.org/yaml-validator) to validate your YAML file.

Step 2: Check Indentation

- **Description:** Ensure indentation is consistent throughout the file.

- **Example:**

```yaml
server:
  host: example.com
  port: 8080
```

Step 3: Verify Data Types

- **Description:** Ensure data types are correctly specified.

- **Error Example:**

```yaml
timeout: "30"  # Should be a number
```

```

- **Correction:**

```yaml
timeout: 30
```

Step 4: Use Debugging Tools

- **Description:** Use debugging tools like `pyyaml` for Python to view and analyze data.

- **Usage Example:**

```python
import yaml

with open('config.yaml', 'r') as file:
    try:
        config = yaml.safe_load(file)
    except yaml.YAMLError as exc:
        print(exc)

## 7.YAML Glossary

**1. Alias**

- **Definition:** A reference to a previously defined node in a YAML document. An alias is used to reuse data without duplication.

- **Example:**

```yaml
default: &default
  timeout: 30
  retries: 5

development:
  <<: *default
  database: dev_db
```

2. Block Mapping

- **Definition:** A YAML mapping style where key-value pairs are written in a block format, with each pair on a new line.

- **Example:**

```yaml
key1: value1

key2: value2
```

3. Block Sequence

- **Definition:** A YAML sequence style where items are listed in a block format, each item on a new line with a leading hyphen.

- **Example:**

```yaml
- item1

- item2

- item3
```

4. Collection

- **Definition:** A general term for YAML data structures that hold multiple items, including sequences (lists) and mappings (dictionaries).

- **Example:**

```yaml
items:
  - apple
  - banana
  - cherry
```

5. Comment

- **Definition:** An annotation in a YAML file that is ignored by parsers, used for documentation or explanation.

- **Example:**

```yaml
# This is a comment
```

key: value

```

**6. Data Type**

- **Definition:** The type of data represented in YAML, such as string, number, boolean, or null.

- **Example:**

```yaml
string: "Hello"

number: 123

boolean: true

null_value: null
```

7. Document

- **Definition:** A single YAML file or a section of a file, marked by a document separator (`---`) when multiple documents are present.
```

- **Example:**

```yaml

---

key: value

...

```

8. Explicit Typing

- **Definition:** Specifying the data type explicitly in YAML using tags.

- **Example:**

```yaml

number: !!int "123"

```

9. Flow Mapping

- **Definition:** A YAML mapping style where key-value pairs are written in a single line, enclosed in curly braces.

- **Example:**

```yaml
{key1: value1, key2: value2}
```

10. Flow Sequence

- **Definition:** A YAML sequence style where items are listed in a single line, enclosed in square brackets.

- **Example:**

```yaml
[item1, item2, item3]
```

11. Inline

- **Definition:** A shorthand notation for writing YAML data structures on a single line, often using flow styles.

- **Example:**

```yaml
```

{name: "John", age: 30}

```

**12. Key**

- **Definition:** The identifier used in YAML mappings to represent the name of a data entry.

- **Example:**

```yaml

key: value

```

13. Mapping

- **Definition:** A YAML data structure that represents key-value pairs, similar to dictionaries in other programming languages.

- **Example:**

```yaml

key1: value1

key2: value2

```

14. Node

- **Definition:** An individual element in a YAML document, which can be a scalar, sequence, or mapping.

- **Example:**

```yaml
- item1  # Sequence node
key: value  # Mapping node
```

15. Scalar

- **Definition:** A single value in YAML, such as a string, number, or boolean.

- **Example:**

```yaml
string: "Hello"
number: 123

boolean: true

```

16. Sequence

- **Definition:** A YAML data structure that represents an ordered list of items.

- **Example:**

```yaml
- item1
- item2
- item3
```

17. Tag

- **Definition:** A type indicator in YAML used to denote the data type of a value.

- **Example:**

```yaml
value: !!int 123

```

18. Value

- **Definition:** The data associated with a key in a YAML mapping or an item in a sequence.

- **Example:**

```yaml

key: value

```

19. YAML Document Separator

- **Definition:** The `---` sequence used to separate multiple YAML documents within a single file.

- **Example:**

```yaml

---

key1: value1

---

key2: value2

```

20. YAML Alias

- **Definition:** A reference to a previously defined node, used to avoid duplication.

- **Example:**

```yaml
default: &default
  timeout: 30
  retries: 5

development:
  <<: *default
  database: dev_db
```

21. YAML Anchor
```

- **Definition:** A marker used to define a reusable reference point in a YAML document.

- **Example:**

```yaml
default: &default
  timeout: 30
```

22. YAML Merge Key

- **Definition:** The `<<` operator used to merge mappings, including inherited values from aliases.

- **Example:**

```yaml
default: &default
  timeout: 30

development:
  <<: *default
```

database: dev_db

```

**23. YAML Plain Style**

- **Definition:** A way of writing scalars without quotes or other delimiters, useful for simple values.

- **Example:**

```yaml
key: value
```

24. YAML Quoted Style

- **Definition:** A way of writing scalars using quotes, either single (`'`) or double (`"`), for more complex strings.

- **Example:**

```yaml
single_quoted: 'Hello'

double_quoted: "Hello"

```

25. YAML Folded Style

- **Definition:** A scalar style where long text blocks are folded into a single line, using the `>` character.

- **Example:**

```yaml
folded: >
  This is a long text
  that will be folded
  into a single line.
```

26. YAML Literal Style

- **Definition:** A scalar style where long text blocks are preserved with newlines, using the `|` character.

- **Example:**

```yaml

literal: |

  This is a long text

  that will be preserved

  with newlines.

```

27. YAML Document Start Marker

- **Definition:** The `---` sequence used at the beginning of a YAML document to indicate the start.

- **Example:**

```yaml
---
key: value
```

28. YAML Document End Marker

- **Definition:** The `...` sequence used to indicate the end of a YAML document.
```

- **Example:**

```yaml
key: value

...
```

This glossary provides a foundational understanding of YAML concepts and terminologies, useful for working with YAML documents and configurations.

Index

www.ingramcontent.com/pod-product-compliance
Lightning Source LLC
Chambersburg PA
CBHW050303230526
45471CB00005B/1995

* 9 7 9 8 3 3 9 0 0 4 1 2 7 *